# THE PENITENTES

### OF THE

# SANGRE de CRISTOS

**BY BILL TATE**

SUNSTONE
PRESS

SANTA FE

Sunstone books may be purchased for educational, business, or sales promotional use. For information please write: Special Markets Department, Sunstone Press, P.O. Box 2321, Santa Fe, New Mexico 87504-2321.
Printed on acid-free paper
∞

Library of Congress Cataloging-in-Publication Data

ON FILE

"For the great ages tragedy is not an expression of despair but the means by which they saved themselves from it. It is a profession of faith."

Krutch

"Great tragedies afford men insights into mysteries otherwise unfathomed."

"Bill Tate is anglo closest to Penitentes."

John MacGregor, Art Editor
Santa Fe New Mexican

"Distinctly not a run of the mill publication. A great deal of research has been done on this book. Valuable for persons interested in this flagellant sect."

Alice Bullock, Book Editor
Santa Fe New Mexican

"A philosophical and rather poetic study of the Penitentes ... based largely on first hand knowledge."

Howard Bryan
Albuquerque Tribune

"It is on the best seller list of southwest books in Albuquerque."

Jim Newton, Book Editor
Albuquerque Journal

"It is well written. The Roadrunner recommends the book to anyone interested in such matters."

Jerry White
Santa Fe News

"Bill Tate is an artist who writes with the touch of a poet."

George Fitzpatrick
New Mexico Magazine

"It is an important contribution to New Mexico literature."

Virginia Mallory
For Frank Waters
New Mexico Arts Commission

"Liked your book very much."

David F. Cargo
Governor

"A sympathetic, unsensational, almost poetic account of the Sect."

Donald M. Powell
Betty Rosenberg
Books of The Southwest

"Bill Tate, Poet, Painter, Philosopher, Poet Laureate of the Penitentes."

Walter Trimble
New Mexico Cultural News
Encanto Magazine

This Book is Dedicated
To
My Daughter
Andrea Maria Teresa
The littlest Penitente of them all

# A PENITENTE OATH

The members of the Pious Fraternity of the County of Taos should know that our intention since old times has been devotion to the Blood of Christ, which was shed to save us sinners, for so did God give His only Son to be offered in sacrifice for sinners. The principal object of our organization is to serve God our Creator in the belief that Jesus Christ is the Saviour of the World according to the teachings of the Holy Gospel; to keep the Ten Commandments of the Law of God, to live humbly; to abjure discord and unjust dealings with our fellow men; to shun saloons and all other temptations the world offers, for "what does it profit a man, if he gain a whole world, but suffers the loss of his own soul;" to act toward one another with charity and mutual love like brothers in Jesus Christ to provide a good example for each other, helping in illness, afflictions and times of need, pardoning one anothers' offences, and mutually tolerating our weaknesses; to follow the humble life given to us as an example by our Lord Jesus Christ, and to recognize and respect each other as members of a body that is Christ Jesus, our Redeemer, and to say as says the Gospel of Saint Matthew, chapter 11, verse 25-26: "I praise Thee, Father, Lord of heaven and earth, that Thou didst hide these things from the wise and prudent, and didst reveal them to the little ones. Yes, Father, for such was Thy good pleasure."

—–O—–

This document dated February 23, 1861, and is published in La Hermanodad, XI, 2 (April, 1889) Pueblo, Colorado. Courtesy Taylor Museum of the Colorado Springs Fine Arts Center.

## PREFACE
## FIRST EDITION

Tragedy is the reenactment of an event of high importance. The Penitentes of the Sangre de Cristos each year during Lent reenact the Passion of Christ.

The Penitentes method of worship through the rite of tragic drama is a way of rendering the incomprehensible comprehensible. It is a manner in which to express the abstract in the concrete, an attempt to make the conceivable perceivable, a striving toward objectivity.

He finds in the unfolding events of the Lenten drama the meaning of the irony and tragedy that he faces in his own life, the unravelling of the inscrutable that he finds all around him in every day events.

Without placing a high value on his own life, the Penitente would find no meaning in his reenacting the tragic events that inevitably led to Calvary. To quote Nietzsche, "they worshipped death so much because they loved life so well." The prerequisite for tragedy is that a high value be placed on human life.

The sorrows and tragedies, and the final agony of Calvary is the supreme epic drama in the Penitente's life, that make his own misfortunes seem less tragic; thus to imitate this sorrowful drama is to attain a kind of atonement for his own inadequacies.

This is the mystery of tragic drama. This is the motivating force of the Penitentes.

BILL TATE
Truchas, N. M.
1966

## PREFACE
## SECOND EDITION

The celebration of the events of Christ's Passion that culminated at Calvary, summons together the most awesome coterie, conspiring to desolate the phyche of the participants in a discordant drama of evil, terror, conflict, pain, regret, defeat, and tragic loss.

While the mystic rites of Lent unfold the Penitente achieves identity with the suffering Christ; transcending the base and mundane of every day events. He is then no longer an ordinary man paralyzed with the inadequacies and frailties of his human condition.

Rarely is the ordinary man given the opportunity to participate in such great events, that are a luxury usually reserved to kings and angels, upon whom such awesome forces are brought to bear, thus achieves for the Penitente a sense of superhuman nobility.

He knows that as he moves forward in the procession that he will be inexorably crushed; that the dark forces of evil will triumph, but he is driven by the grandeur and pageantry while they sing and march toward defeat, with their swaying lanterns, whirring matracas, the blowing of flutes, and the fluttering robes of the Cristo toward inevitable pain and death at Calvario, but it is his abiding faith and the magnitude of that defeat that is sublime, and wins our admiration and fills us with awe, and causes us to reach aesthetic heights. He has surrendered to the inevitability of the tragic event, and our eyes are filled with tears of rapture when we achieve awareness of the awesome powers with which he is faced, but through his faith he remains sublime in his downfall.

The tragedy of Calvary has made heroes out of the survivors. The Penitente has triumphed over pain and defeat, and on Easter Sunday he is allowed to share with his Saviour the joys and the triumph of the resurrection.

How otherwise are we to measure the victory gained by the resurrection, if it has not come out of sorrow and defeat, yes, even death?

Bill Tate, Truchas, N. M. 1967

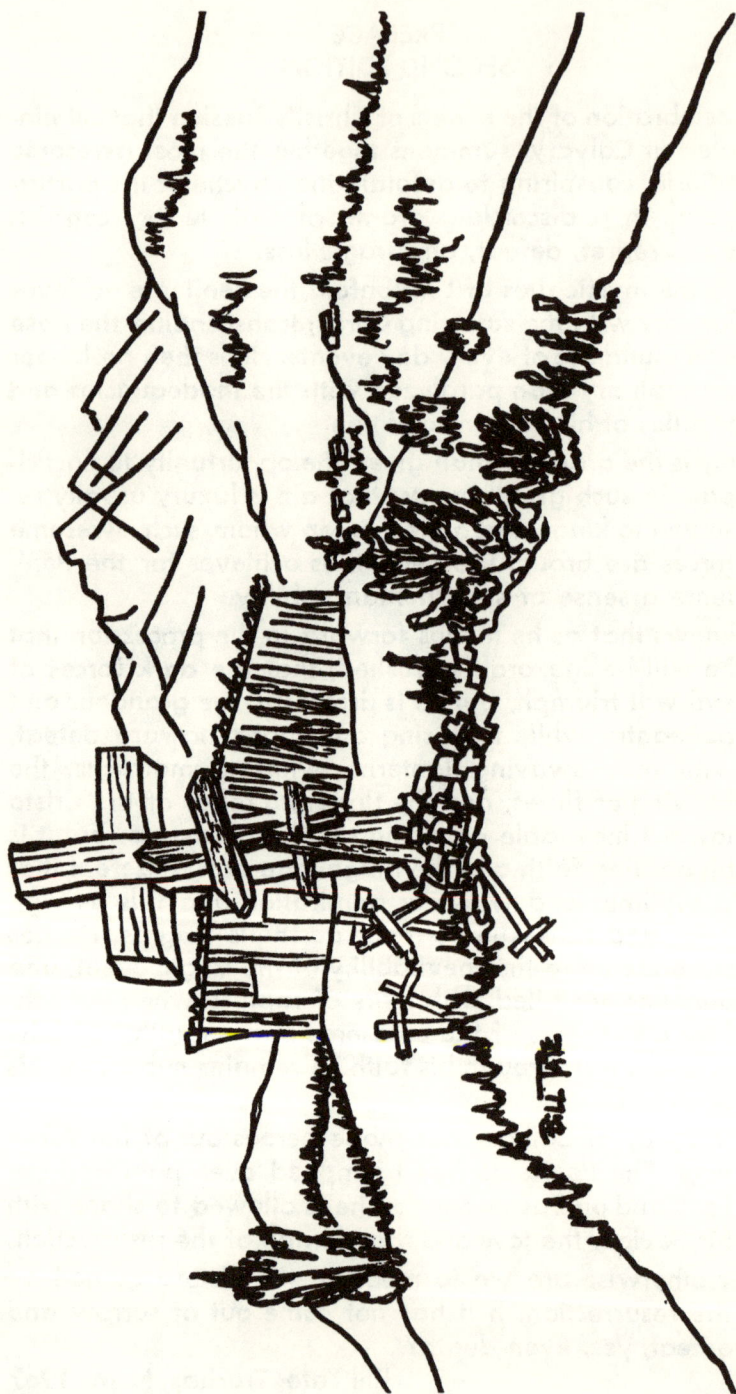

CALVARIO IN TRUCHAS

To be a Penitente
is to be in love.
To be in Love is tragedy.
The Penitente is in love
with the suffering Christ.
He seeks with fury
To assuage his sorrows
by imitation; an illusion
begetting disillusion.
In his desolation
Love and Death become one.
He seeks identity by
Dissolution of his own identity,
The at onement of love and death,
A subjective metamorphosis,
aspiring to the objective;
Thus seeking something beyond;
Discovering that he perpetuates himself
on earth only if he dies;
To yield his life up to another
for only through another
can he renew his life
for when bodies are united by pleasure
their souls are united by pain.
In the depths of his love
He sounds the depths of his own misery.
This is the secret of the Penitente.
BILL TATE • TRUCHAS • AUGUST • 1969

PROCESSION

# INTRODUCTION

Much has been said and written about the Penitentes[1] of the Upper Rio Grande Region of Northern New Mexico and Southern Colorado, most of which has been colored by the prejudices and preconceived notions of the reporters. Much more is completely untrue.

I live among the Penitentes in the village of Las Truchas,[2] New Mexico, a Spanish American community high on the ramparts of the Sangre de Cristo[3] Mountains, at the foot of the towering Truchas Peaks, the triple crowns of Nueva Espana.

I have no portfolio to be their apologist or oracle, but I have taken it upon myself to portray and to clarify who the Penitentes are, what they do, and why, as lucidly and objectively as is possible.

It is important that I achieve my purpose, because I believe that the Penitentes of this region are an important part of our American Heritage. They are the only existing theological and cultural folk expression in America of the ancient world, a link between the old and the new.

Because of the nature of the material, very little testimony is available—even less that can be verified. The rest must be left to conjecture. Therefore the validity of the evidence is dependent upon direct observation and participation. I have done both.

I don't believe that one can probe the profundity and mystery of a drama by catching a part of the 3rd act, or be moved by a liturgy by watching it from afar. To achieve the desired enlightenment requires involvement, not by the clock or calendar, but as an unending, continuing, all permeating part of ones' life. The Penitentes are an important part of mine.

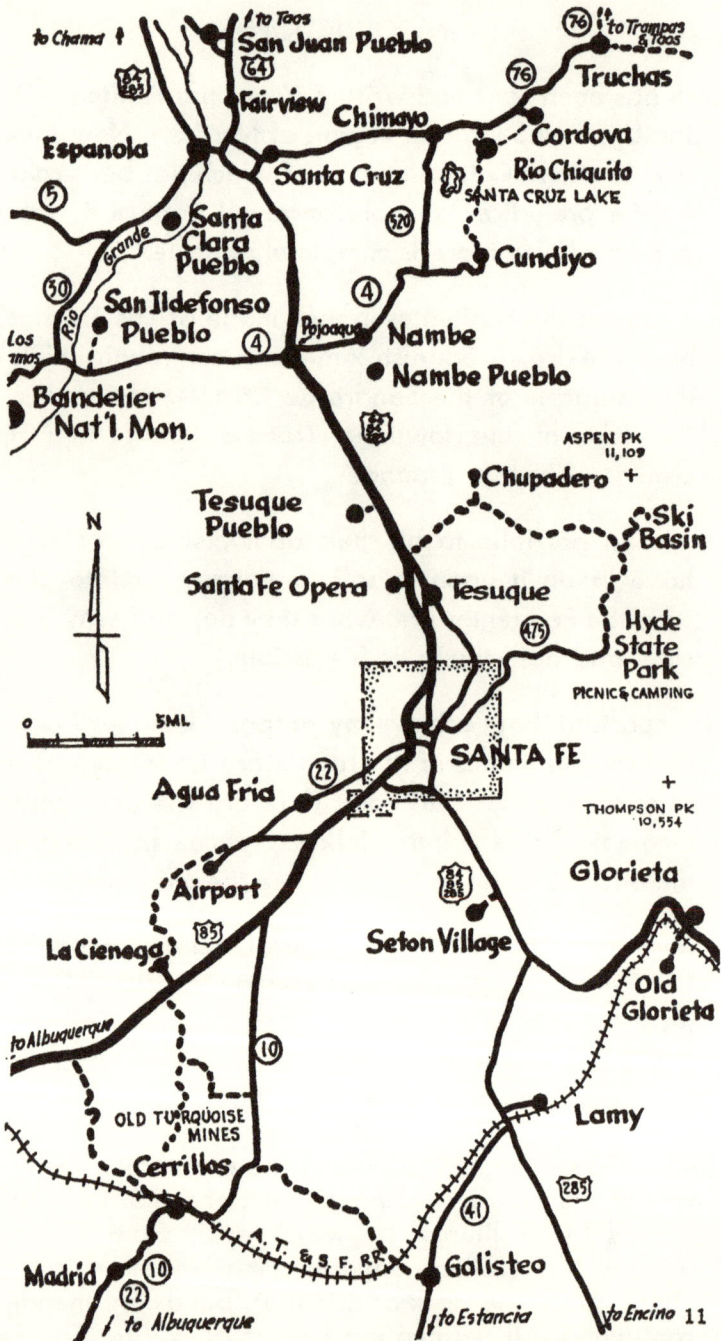

to Chama †

to Taos

San Juan Pueblo

285

64

Fairview

Chimayo

76

to Trampas & Taos

76

Truchas

Cordova

Espanola

Santa Cruz

Rio Chiquito

SANTA CRUZ LAKE

5

Santa
Clara
Pueblo

520

Grande

Cundiyo

30

San Ildefonso
Pueblo

Rio

4

Pojoaque

Nambe

Los
mos

4

Nambe Pueblo

Bandelier
Nat'l. Mon.

ASPEN PK
11,109

Chupadero +

N

Tesuque
Pueblo

Ski
Basin

Santa Fe Opera

Tesuque

Hyde
State
Park

475

0        5 ML

PICNIC & CAMPING

Agua Fria

22

SANTA FE

+

THOMPSON PK
10,554

Airport

Glorieta

85

La Cienega

Seton Village

Old
Glorieta

to Albuquerque

10

Lamy

OLD TURQUOISE
MINES

285

Cerrillos

41

A. T. & S. F. R.R.

Madrid

10

22

to Albuquerque

Galisteo

to Estancia

to Encino  11

MAP BY WALTER DAWLEY

9

# I

## WHO ARE THE PENITENTES?

The Penitentes are a secret(4) and sacred Spanish-American brotherhood who live in the mountains of Northern New Mexico and Southern Colorado, who have pledged themselves to Christian devotions without completely withdrawing from the daily world. They have dedicated themselves in rememberance that Christ was condemned, crucified, and died on the cross for the salvation of mankind, and the expiation of his sins.

Their devotions are observed usually in secret because the Penitentes believe that worship is a private matter, and that one should not seek approbation for ones sacred endeavors.

The Penitente liturgy consists mainly of prayers called rosarios,(5) rapturous songs called alabados(6) and processions.

The principal events on the Penitente calendar occur during Lent, primarily during Holy Week called Semana Santa,(7) beginning on Wednesday, and culminating Saturday morning before Easter, and in July when the Carmelites hold a nine day novena for Our Lady of Mt. Carmel.

They practice their worship by reenacting the events that led to Christ's passion, crucifixion and entombment, much like the Greeks who by tragic drama celebrated the sacred rituals of their gods.

It is inherent in the Spanish mystique to believe that through mystery and tragedy will transcendental beauty and nobility emerge, because as surely as the warm sun follows the rain, out of tragedy will follow ecstacy.

The Penitentes are the descendants of the vanguard of Spanish colonists who settled in the highlands of Northern New Mexico and Southern Colorado during the floodtide of Spanish colonization.

As the occupation receded and Mexico subsequently achieved her independence from Spain, the representatives of both Church and Government were ordered by the Crown of Spain to return to the homeland from Nueva Espana, leaving the people to their own resources, limited as these must have been in those times.

Inexorably it devolved upon the Penitentes to become the guardians of the Faith, to nurture it, and keep it alive. As the churches fell into neglect and disrepair, the moradas grew and flourished.

The Morada(8) became the town hall and temple. Those who were not members in those days were certainly the exception and not the rule. These conditions prevailed until the arrival of Archbishop Lamy in 1851,(9) and the subsequent revival of Catholic orthodoxy. To a degree they continue to prevail in the more isolated areas of Northern New Mexico to this very day.

The Penitentes of today are farmers, laborers, and oftentimes public officials. Your next door neighbor may be a Penitente, if you live in Northern New Mexico.

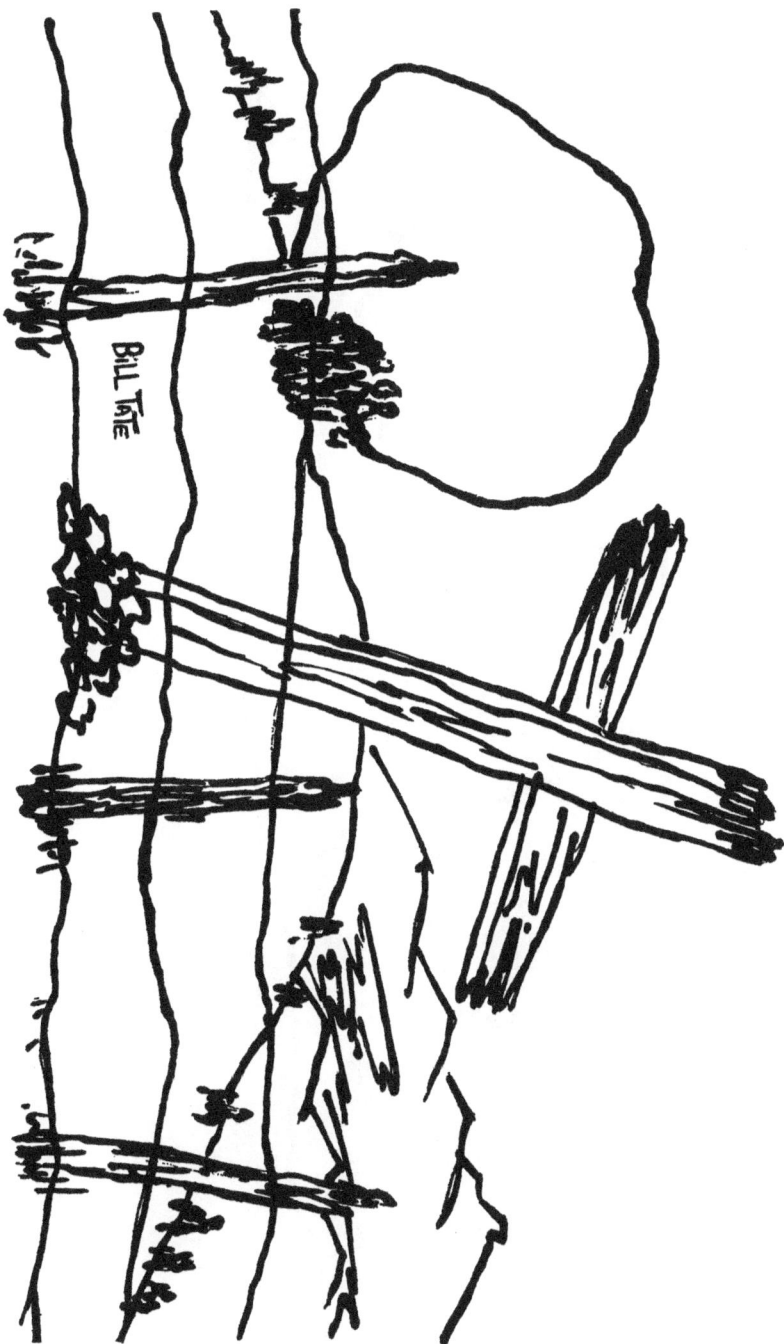

BILL TATE

PROCESSION TO CALVARIO

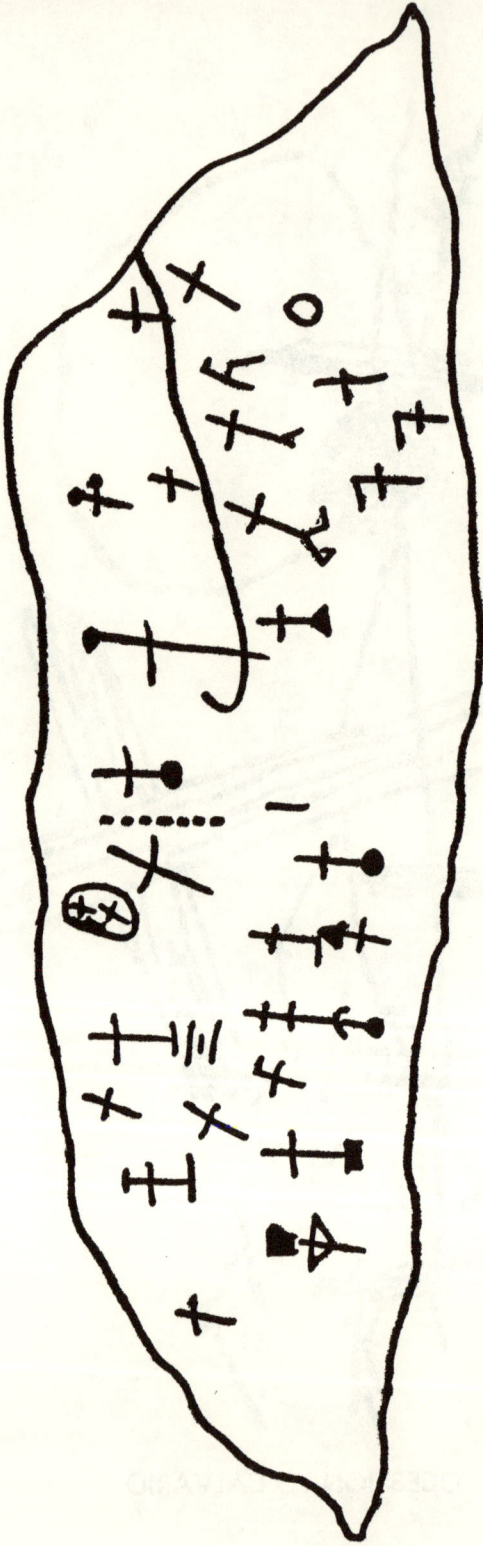

Petroglyphs, believed to record a Penitente ritual and subsequent procession to Calvario.

Bill Tate

# II

## THE ORIGIN OF THE PENITENTES

Much has been said, but little is known about the origin of
the Penitentes. Each historian, it seems, has his own
particular version of when and where they came from,
contingent upon what perspective he views them.
Due to the obvious lack of concurrence, it must be considered that there are no "facts" as such.

Some trace them to the flagellant sect of the 3rd Order of
St. Francis,[10] because much of their ritual was evi-
dently assimilated from the early day Franciscans, the
first religious leaders of Nueva Espana, but this need
not be the whole story. They may well go back earlier
that.

Through the ages man has utilized tragic drama as a means of catharsis and expiation.(11) We witness this in the songs of Homer, the dramas of Aeschylus and Euripides.

Identity and transcendence have been achieved through imitation and representation since the dawn of human history. This phenomenon perhaps antedates the Cro-Magnon paintings in the caves of Altamira in Santander, also the eagle and buffalo dances of the Pueblo Indians.

Such rites are not confined to a particular place in geography, but exist over the entire surface of the earth.

The magic that lies behind the imitation of Christ's Passion and subsequent Resurrection presumes the expiation of man's sins, his inexorable death, his subsequent rising and his sharing a seat in paradise.

Understanding this, one may conclude, that these rites and aspirations have been germaine to most cultures since earliest history, and that the Penitentes represent a continuation of these rituals until the present time.

To arrive at this conclusion would necessarily require some perspective of Spanish history during the time of the conquest and colonization of Spanish America.(12)

Ferdinand of Old Castile was confirmed by Alexander VI, the Spanish Pope as "The Catholic King" and was reigning during the consummation of medievalism in Europe. The Spanish Church was wealthy and powerful at this time, because the people were not only intensely religious, but it was also a national institution, and the Crown was supreme, and had the Inquisition under its control.

Cut off from the sea on all sides, and still engaged in the bitter struggle with the Moors, Old Castile still preserved through the era of Spanish American colonization the medieval features of its culture.

Castilian was the literary language of Spain, and consequently of Spanish America as well. Old Castile was the matrix out of which the religiosity of the early colonists of Nueva España was formed.

15

It was during this time in Old Castile that Santa Teresa(13) de Avila instituted the reforms of the Carmelites(14) which spread throughout Spanish America. She wrote the Libro de su Vida and Libro de las Moradas; thus extending the philosophical limits of the Spanish language and the embryonic probing of the subconcious.

San Juan de la Cruz de los Caballeros(15) also of Avila in Old Castile was the author of symbolistic hymns and poetry that achieved the epitome of rapturous ecstacy. He was also a member of the Carmelites and was imprisoned for his unorthodox teachings and religious practices, but even so, exercised considerable influence on the subconcious of the early explorers and settlers of Nueva España.

This is the literary and religious heritage of the Penitentes, that has been carried down by them to the present day.

This has been possible because Nueva España at that time was as isolated from the Old World as the other planets of our solar system are from us today. Thus the Mountain People of Northern New Mexico retained, with little adulteration the rituals and faith of her Spanish forebearers in Old Castile.(16)

There were many secularist years after Mexico gained her independence from Spain. During these years, there were few, if any, representatives of the Church in the Northern New Mexico mountain villages. Because of this, the people's only religious expression was through the rituals of the Penitentes. This circumstance continued until long after the American invasion by General Kearney, who brought with him an alien anglo-protestant theology.

After the troops of the United States secured the northern region of New Mexico, the Church in the person of Archbishop Lamy made its reentry into the area. Once again these people were urged to return to the rites of the Roman Catholic Church.

However, because of their isolation from population centers and routes of commerce, as well as the strong hold their traditions had on them, these deeply religious people continued to retain the rites of the Penitentes, practicing them under the most difficult circumstances. For this they were condemned and ostracised, both by an unsympathetic church and government. It was for these reasons that the Penitentes were compelled to go more or less underground.

Because of the encroachments and demands of modern society, all that remains today are only the vestiges of these rituals that at one time played such a large part in the lives of the people that inhabited the valleys and the hidden villages in the highlands of the Sangre de Cristos.

Economics and social convention are strangling the life out of what little is left of these practices and traditions that have been germaine to their culture since the beginning of their odyssey in Old Castile. ,

Bid farewell to the processions and the songs that have fulfilled the vital essence of the Penitente psyche for so many generations, for though the Alabados may disappear like the wind into the past, but like the wind which no one has ever seen, but only has heard, his spirit will still ask with yearning, "What does it say?" He will sense the answer, but go unknowing.

VIA DOLOROSA

NIGHT CHANT

19

# III

## THE CARMELITES

Very little has been written about the Lady's Order of the Penitentes, known as the Carmelites, even though they are a vital and active part of the society.

It is quite possible that they antedate the Penitentes by many centuries. It is legendary that the Carmelites antedate the Birth of Christ, and that they celebrated their rituals on Mt. Carmel in the Holy Land back to the days of the prophets. It is said that Mary, the Mother of Jesus attended services there, and was pledged as a member, and that St. Peter delivered a sermon on Mt. Carmel to them on Pentecost, and also joined them, as well as the other apostles. Among their membership were believed to be the Essenes.

The Carmelites are one of the mysteries of history, and are closely analagous to the Franciscans, as are the Penitentes.

In the early part of the 13th century the Carmelites became a part of the 3rd Order of St. Francis[17] and were known as The Sisters of Penance, Mt. Carmel in Palestine no longer being a safe abode for them.

In Avila in Old Castile Santa Teresa along with San Juan de la Cruz de Los Caballeros during the 16th Century instituted numerous reforms of the Carmelites. They were brought to Spanish America by the Conquistadores.

In the absence of written records, one has to resort only to legends, but the fragments that have been pieced together seem to substantiate these legends with some validity.

During the middle of July the Carmelites hold daily services, including a procession, to celebrate the Feast of Our Lady of Carmel. These services last for nine days.

During Lent they sing the Stations of the Cross every Friday afternoon in the Old Church of Truchas, and also every day from Palm Sunday through Good Friday.

On the morning of Good Friday, the Carmelites carry the Mater Dolorosa during the Encuentro, a profound and sorrowful occasion, perhaps the most meaningful and beautiful service held by the Penitentes in their rituals during Holy Week. This is when the Holy Mother bids Her Son farewell, before His departure to Calvary.

The Carmelites also sing in processions and during the rituals at velorios, the services held for a member when he dies. These last for 72 hours, giving untold consolation to the survivors.

They are responsible for the upkeep of the Old Church in Truchas, and help the men with different duties in the Morada, and other tasks of the Order.

Although their rituals are not as dramatic as are the men's, their role is every bit as important and satisfying.

BETRAYED AND SCOURGED

# Archbishop Grants Church Blessing To Penitente Order in New Mexico

Archbishop Edwin V. Byrne today, in a declaration on the status of the Penitentes, granted this order the Catholic church's blessing and protection, "if the Brethren proceed with moderation and privately under our supervision."

Miguel Archibeque and leaders of the Hermanos have acted to rid them of "excesses and abuses" which have occurred in their practices in past years, the metropolitan says. However, "there are still instances of individual bad lives, as in other societies, and this or that group still makes itself a political football, thus giving a bad name to the Brethren."

Declaring the order's aim is corporal and spiritual penance, he declares such acts "after abolishing whatever excess or abuse there might have been, are not acts of sadism or masochism . . . not so severe or cruel as to injure one's health."

Frowning upon what has been called "Penitente hunting," the archbishop says no polite or cultured person should try to spy upon their meetings.

His statement follows in full:

It has become necessary for us to make a definite declaration regarding the Brothers of Jesus of Nazareth (commonly called the Penitentes), in order to clarify their status both to Catholics as well as to non-Catholics.

These Brothers or Brethren constitute a pious association of men joined in charity to commemorate the passion and death of the Redeemer. This society, like many others in the Catholic church, is part of that church and therefore deserves her protection and guidance so long as it keeps and practices the teachings of the Church.

Its origin is obscure in history. It seems that it began somewhere in the beginnings of the last century when the Franciscan padres left New Mexico by order of the new government of Mexico. No other priests were sent to take their place. Groups among the faithful tried to keep up Catholic practices without priestly guidance, and though certain excesses crept in, it is to these groups of penitential brethren that we owe, in a manner, the preservation of the faith in those hard and trying times.

But why do we make this declaration now? Precisely because many, even Catholics, harbor an erroneous idea concerning this association. It cannot be denied that the association itself is at fault because of certain excesses and abuses in the past. There are still scattered instances of individual bad lives, as in other societies, and this or that group still makes of itself a political football, thus giving a bad name to the Brethren.

However, moved by the admirable zeal of Mr. Miguel Archibeque, who at cost of great personal sacrifice

(Continued on Page Seven)

has conferred with heads and important members (Hermanos mayores), in order to abolish any abuse, there might be and so place the association definitely under the guidance and protection of the Catholic church which they love so much, I, as archbishop of Santa Fe, take them under my supervision to guide them according to directions already accepted by them, and to protect them from ill-instructed persons who consider them as objects of curiosity or ridicule.

Therefore, I declare:

1. That the Association of Hermanos de Nuestro Senor Jesus Nazareno is not a fanatical sect apart from the church, as some seem to think, but an association of Catholic men united together in love for the passion and death of our Blessed Lord and Saviour;

2. That the end of this society is to do corporal and spiritual penance, for the saying of our Lord concerning the necessity of penance for salvation is just as true now as it was centuries ago, and therefore there should be no shameful connotation attached to the word penitent; (The saints, like the humble and sweet St. Francis of Assisi, loved by the wild birds and beasts, and whom the whole world still loves and admires, practiced many penances. The Third Order, which he founded for lay people in the world, he himself called "the Order of Penance." And this confirms us in the opinion that the Hermanos are descended from those Tertiaries founded here by the Franciscans in centuries gone by. Certainly, there is no connection, as some writers claim, between the Hermanos and those fanatical sects of Flagellants in medieval times);

3. That these acts of penance, after abolishing whatever excess or abuse there might have been, are not acts of sadism or masochism, as modern wise men wish to say in these days, softened by luxury and comfort; and that they are not so severe or cruel as to injure one's health, for then they would be sins and not acts of virtue; and that these penances must be done in private to avoid scandal, because Christian penance is of itself private and not like that of the Pharisees; hence it follows, that no individual, be he Catholic or not, should interfere with their meetings, just as no one who deems himself polite or cultured would try to break in or spy on the meetings of societies to which he does not belong;

4. That we have the authority and power to suppress this association, just as we can and must suppress any other pious association in the church which goes counter to, or exceeds, the laws of God and His church, or the discipline of reason. But if the Brethren proceed with moderation and privately and under our supervision, meanwhile giving a good example to all as Catholics and citizens, they have our blessing and protection.

Newspaper account of decree of Archbishop Edwin V. Bryne, accepting the Penitentes into the Church. It requires certain concessions by the Penitentes; condemns "Penitente Hunters".

# IV

## THE ATTITUDE OF THE CHURCH

Since the arrival of Archbishop Lamy in 1851, and the subsequent establishment of an Archbishopric in Santa Fe, the Roman Catholic Church has continually sustained a campaign designed to suppress the Penitentes, even though it was they who had nurtured and kept alive the Faith through the long secular years.

It wasn't until the reign of the late Archbishop Edwin Byrne that a compromise was finally achieved in 1947. The Penitentes were permitted to participate in the affairs of the Morada, provided they follow certain guidelines as set down by the Church.

Even though the attitude of the Church has softened with the years, apparently the attitudes of the parish priests have not necessarily changed. This is understandable because the priests have to deal with the Penitentes more directly. It must be difficult to administer a parish wherein a portion of the parishioners have outside religious commitments.

Apparently the zeal and esoteric nature of the Penitentes' rituals confounds or embarasses some of the priests and their congregations in the villages where the Penitentes predominate; as one priest so aptly put it, "It gives scandal to the Church!"

The present Archbishop has made no public pronouncements regarding the Penitentes; so apparently a live and let live attitude prevails up to this writing.

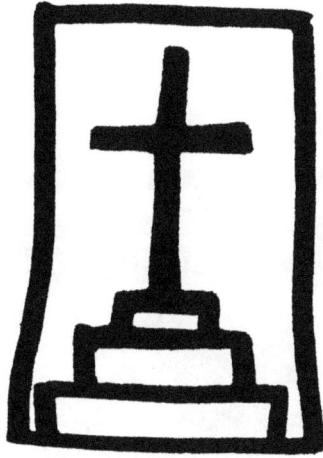

# V

## THE FUTURE OF THE PENITENTES

The future of the Penitentes is tenuous and in doubt; however, each year during Holy Week in the Morada, and in the processions, one sees new faces. How long this can continue under the pressures of modern society one can only surmise.

Today the youth of the Spanish villages of the Sangre de Cristos are moving away to the metropolitan areas to complete their educations and to seek work.

The Great Society with the Job Corps and other economic and educational inducements will undoubtedly make even deeper inroads into the Penitentes' membership.

It is very unlikely that these young people when they become involved with the social structure of the metropolitan areas and suburbia will ever return to the old ways of their fathers.

Although the Penitentes are still vital and active at the present time, and they are continuing to take in new members, their numbers are decreasing. It is inevitable that they will gradually fade away into the misty realm of legend and history.

*Esta vida es un engaño,*
*y no tiene otro desvelo,..*

## LA CARRETA DE LA MUERTE

# VI

## THE ART OF THE PENITENTES

No other art form of any other people since the middle
Ages or the Byzantine better portrays the profundity of
emotion or the depth of human religious expression
than does the sacred art of the Penitentes of Northern
New Mexico.[18]

It embodies not only the mood of medievalism but the as-
ceticism of El Greco, the grief imbued in the Gothic,
and the Miserere of Rouault, as well as the stark sim-
pilcity of the frescoes in the catacombs beneath Rome,
that were tantamount to prayers and offerings for the
salvation of the deceased.

The sacred folk art of these people, in all its deceiving
simplicity, best portrays the awful impact of Christ's
pilgrimage and His agonizing ascent to Calvary in a
fashion captured perhaps only by Gruenwalt.

Penitente art represents the honest uninhibited religious expression of a simple people steeped in a deep religious tradition, a people who have suffered the terrible isolation and the hostile environment of the high plateaus of the Sangre de Cristos, with their tenuous existence dependent upon a short and fitful growing season, a people whose life and death were fused in a fatal alliance, making it easy to identify themselves with the suffering and dying Christ.

Plastic forms of religious representation known as santos are divided into three general categories. These include the tin frames in which religious pictures are placed.

They are usually made from tin cans, many of which retain the imprint of the manufacturer of the product. Their intricate designs were fashioned by using leather dies, as well as those used in the manufacture of Indian jewelry. They can be quite ornate, and to the untrained eye resemble silver.

The pictures that were placed in them were taken from old prayer books, and many of them were gravure prints brought to New Mexico by the traders over the Santa Fe Trail. Many of these were printed in France and Germany, and many by Currier and Ives, who printed them especially for trade with the inhabitants of Spanish America. The most famous subjects represented were Christ on the Cross, The Virgin of Guadalupe and the Santo Nino.

Other Santos were painted on wood coated with gesso, using mostly vegetable dies for color. These are called retablos.

Figures in the round are known as bultos, the highest expression of which are the Cristos, almost life sized figures of Christ used in the processions and other ceremonies. They are dramatic and imposing. In the making of the Cristo, the Penitente santero poured forth the total of his emotions and artistic genius.

The Penitentes created an art form designed to provoke feeling, to achieve identity, and to assure transcendance, to live with, to share in their sufferings and joys; an art form in its most noble manifestation.

> "The Russian icon is one of the highest forms of artistic expression in the world ... It is a unique phenomena in the history of painting. They bequeathed to us priceless gifts whose beauty is filled with a profound meaning.
>
> These icons of early Russia have revealed man's own inner world, his purity, and nobility of soul, his readiness for sacrifice, and the depth of his thought and feeling.
>
> My generation has been lucky enough to be the first to discover the real Russian icon, beneath the coats of varnish and later inscriptions which obscured it, and reveal to the world a brilliant art that enthralls us by the exquisite harmony of its coloring, the easy flow of its lines, and the deeply spiritual significance of its imagery."
>
> By Igor Grabar
> People's Painter, USSR

These are truths that are equally applicable to New Mexico's iconography, perhaps even more so because Russia's craft, though resembling that of ours, was produced by professional painters more or less under the direction of the Church, whereas ours was the free expression of the individual santero uninhibited by authority, and are the honest expressions of his own inner consciousness, and naive interpretations of the legends as handed down by his own forebearers.

Today these beautiful and anthropomorphic pieces are finding their way into private homes as the prizes of collectors or hidden in the dark recesses in the basements of museums, while being rapidly replaced in the Moradas and the churches by plaster, plastic and chrome effigies so outrageously vulgar in taste that only the priests and members could be their apologists.

MORADA IN TRUCHAS

Bill Tate

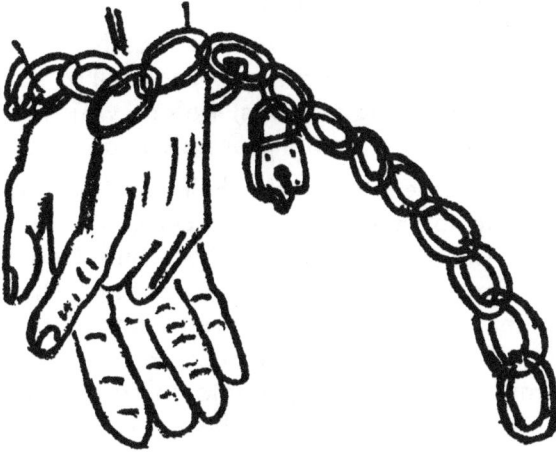

# VII

## ARCHITECTURE — THE MORADA

The architecture of the Penitentes is best expressed in the design and layout of the Morada. If it is true that architecture is the mother of the arts, best relating the nature, environment, and the purpose of a people, then the Morada is the one structure in a Spanish village that fulfills these aesthetic prerequisites.

The Penitente Morada is usually situated in a prominent location, alone, like a monument and oftentimes within the community cemetery.[20]

It is easy to identify, because it is usually long and low, close to the earth. Its length usually several times its width, shaped not unlike a coffin. Its massive walls are of hand textured adobe, giving the structure a unique organic sculptured quality. It is the essence of simplicity in design.

There are seldom any windows, but if there are, they are invariably quite small, much like gun ports. Obviously they were recessed deeply into the walls to give only a minimum of light. The door, though heavily timbered, is proportionately small.

Opposite the entrance is usually a massive cross, known as a "calvario",(21) a sun and snow silvered cenotaph of ancient hand adzed logs, before which outdoor rituals are performed and processions are assembled.

Unlike great cathedrals with their vaulted domes and triumphant towers designed to celebrate the victory of the risen Christ, the ascended Lord and King, presiding on the Throne of God with the earth as His footstool, with their worshipping congregations singing out Te Deums and Hallelujahs, echoing to the very heavens, the simple and silent Penitente Morada stands like a stark sarcophagus to house the Cristo, Ecce Homo, the suffering Christ of the Passion, a cimmerian chamber wherein to pray, and to contemplate the irony of His tragic life . and death; to identify with His suffering and sacrifice, hoping to achieve atonement for all of mankind by imitation of His tragedy. His indignities and scourging in the court of Caiaphus, His humiliation because of the vacilations of Pilate, His inexorable struggle to Calvary, the enormity and cruelty of His crucifixion, and consequent liberation by death, and His subsequent descent into Purgatorio, the rending earthquake, and the awful silence when the centurions stood vigil with their swaying lanterns during that interminable night; where there are no Easters.

The Morada was built to do with the events and artifacts that give character and meaning to that for which liturgical architecture was intended; for without tragedy there could be no triumph. It is here in the dark recesses of the Morada that a basic people have fathomed the mystery of basic faith, the genesis of Christian philosophy.

With this in mind, the Morada is architecturally the quintessence of liturgical exactitude. It is here that the mood has been established.

Bill Thie

ON A HILL FAR AWAY

Actual Penitente Alabados, photographed from a Penitente songbook. Rezadors copy these from books of elders; thus are handed down from one to the other. Writing and verbiage remain archaic, even though modifications are made in each copying. How much present day Alabados resemble "original" Alabados is not known.

# VIII

### PENITENTE MUSIC

Very little of the Penitente ritual is performed without music. The Penitente's melancholy songs are heard on the wind, wafting from the Morada during the hours of the day and night, during different times of the year, and when anyone dies.

Like the Penitentes themselves, very little is known about the origins of the songs. Some say that they remind them of the old Jewish canticles, but others say that they sound much like the music heard in the mosques of Tangiers and Morocco.

The Gregorian chants are much too sophisticated and too European to be considered for attribution. Santa Teresa and San Juan de la Cruz wrote many exalted poems and hymns for the Carmelites in the 16th Century. Many of the Alabados could be the descended versions of these.

The Moors of Old Castile could have influenced to a considerable degree their haunting tones. The Cantors in their worship in the Synagogues must have contributed too, because they were very much a part of the religious life of Old Castile.

Every Penitente sings from a small book, much like the old "time books". The novitiate upon joining the Penitentes copies the songs from the book of the village rezador, and thus the songs go on and on, with the modifications made in the copying.

The principal Penitente instruments consist of flutes, clackers, matracas,(24) and occasionally a drum. The flute has been used since the earliest times to imitate the emotions of higher personages in tragedies. They are mentioned as having been used in this way in Aristotle's Poetics, and were used to accompany Pindar in the singing of his odes, and for the dithyrambs of the Dionysians. The songs of the flute seem to be ammytrical to the singing. The sadder the occasion the more pronounced the dissonance. If one has ever heard the wailing of the flute of the Penitentes, it will haunt his psyche always, and cause him to yearn, wherever he may be to hear it over and over again.

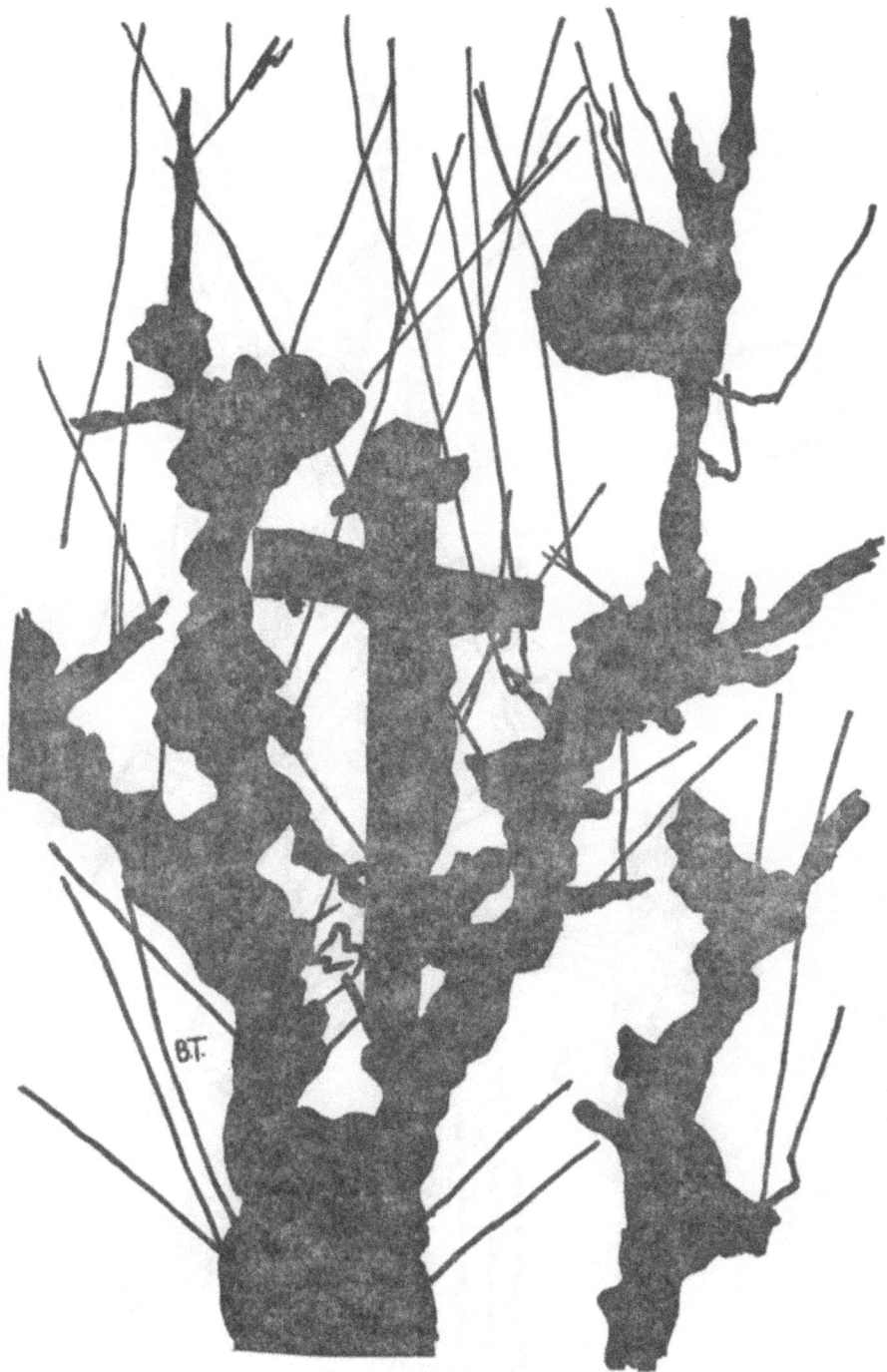

THE CRUCIFIXION

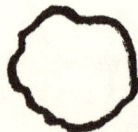

DESCENT FROM CALVARIO

# IX

## THE RITUALS OF THE PENITENTES

Rouault could have come from Truchas. Although he was
European, he best expressed the mood of Truchas and
her Penitentes in his "Miserere", more than has any
other artist.

To help better understand these fervently religious people
one should be familiar with the works of Rouault, Niet-
zche, Aeschylus, and Euripides, as well as Aristotle's
Poetics, and Donaldson.

The tradition of identity by imitation, and the catharsis
achieved in the Greek drama closely parallel the experience of participating in the Penitente rituals.

It is to have drunk the narcotic drought of the Orphic gods
to the accompaniment of their night songs deep in the
mountain forests; to have visited Dante's Purgatorio,
and to have knelt at Fino-Slavic altars.

The blue and silver crescent of the Truchas Peaks, forming a natural amphitheatre at the foot of the Santa Cruz de las Sierras,[22] is the perfect setting for the reenactment of Christ's Passion; the perfect mirror for mankind's greatest drama.

The Penitente is the archtype of suffering humanity, embodying man's deepest and most intense emotions, while at the same time ecstatically enraptured by his close proximity to the suffering Christ.

He has become His suffering and sympathetic companion, a dramatic protophenomena who is transformed before one's very eyes, a demigod who has taken possession of another body and another character, epidemically manifesting himself in grand metamorphosis.

The tragic chorus catalysis a narcosis on transformed beings, while they whir their matracas and blow their pipes down the winding road, etched in space, while marching on the precipice toward the towering indigo Truchas Peaks, against the raging winds in the cold moonlight, accompanied by the clanking of dragging chains, and swinging their torches and lanterns in accompaniment.

The whole drama bespeaks enchantment and becomes a work of art, indeed a strange and fearful drama.

## THE LAST SUPPER
### PART 1

It was in the Morada shortly after midnight Holy Thursday morning. The Penitentes formed a semicircle around us, holding upright large crosses at least seven feet high. Their classic El Greco-like features were gently outlined in the soft vermillion glow of the candles they held in their hands.

The Penitentes had the sad and downcast look of men who were about to make the supreme sacrifice, as they sung the Alabados, Orphic hymns to the dying Christ.

The groaning table was heaped with plates of food; — fish, vegetables, and desserts. The cold and bitter wind was howling outside. A guard stood at the heavy timbered door of the Morada, occasionally opening it, probing the darkness with his powerful flashlight, as though expecting to find some unseen prowler or intruder.

Everybody ate with gusto in spite of the fact that the event was to celebrate one of history's saddest events, The Last Supper.(23) This was the first of many events that would culminate in the most terrifying moment of all, His crucifixion and death, and subsequent descent into Purgatorio.

The people of the village had been invited to the Morada to join together in remembrance of the sad occasion when the Lord last met with His apostles and foretold the forboding sequence of events that were to culminate at Calvary.

The evening had begun with prayers and singing in the little chapel, in the nave of the Morada, not unlike the Lord that fatal night at Gethsemane.


## ENCUENTRO

## PART II

Good Friday morning we gathered in the patio of the old Truchas church. In the distance we could hear the mournful voices of the Carmelites as they slowly wended their sorrowful way through the narrow lanes between the houses, carrying with them the Mater Dolorosa (The Mother of Sorrows), the Mother of the soon to be crucified Christ.

Against the broad south wall of the church, as though it was the wailing wall of Jerusalem, the Carmelites sang of the tragic loss of Her Son, pouring into their lament the great grief of all mothers in all times everywhere, whose sons had given their lives for aspirations, otherwise unattainable except by making the supreme sacrifice, even though perhaps beyond their own comprehension.

Down the main road came the Penitentes bearing on their shoulders a platform upon which stood, in abject humility the Cristo clothed in purple as described in Scripture. He was blindfolded with a black cloth, and a noose of frayed halyard was firmly secured around His neck, Ecce Homo, The Son, a condemned man about to die.

The Penitentes were sadly blowing their pipes in so solitary a fashion that each time they are heard, their mournful wails recall from the subsconscious the nostalgia of an event so remote and unremembered, yet so provocative that one is almost overcome with grief, evoking a deep inner longing reaching far into ones' historic subconscious.

The roaring matracas whirred ominously, fortelling impending doom, and the clackers ticked out the terminating heart beats of the condemned.

The Carmelites entered from the back of the church, and went into the patio. The Penitentes came through the front gate. For the first time since the beginning of His long ordeal, Mother and Son meet before the large Calvario. There was an interminable period of suspense, punctuated by the singing of the melancholy Alabados, that wafted on the crisp morning breeze. Without warning the Mother and Son fell into one another's arms at right angles to each other. Mother and Son, reliving a lifetime of dreams and memories, in one giant and grotesque embrace, forming a cross of black and purple.

There was a cry of awe and profound sorrow by the onlookers as the Mother and Son held their awkward position for what seemed an eternity. It was the Mother and Her God-Son, a God-Man about to become a Man-God bidding farewell, an occasion for the greatest grief ever experienced by a mother for her son. The cool breeze fluttered their whispering gowns, echoed by the lamenting flutes, and the sobbing songs of the celebrants.

## TINIEBLAS

## PART III

Late that night the Penitentes marched into the old candle-lit church, their matracas whirring, and pipes blowing shrilly. They marched straight up to the altar and stopped. The rezador(25) dropped out of the formation and walked onto the altar, and poured forth his grief and heart in song. The Penitente brothers gave their responses on bended knees antiphonically. Their eyes and faces were heavy and haggard with weariness from days and nights of processions and vigils. Now was the time for the Tinieblas.

Three of the brothers joined the rezador by singing together at the left of the altar. An elder brother took a seat on the altar to the right, and another took a place to the left as the Alabados were being sung. Each of the thirteen candles, seven on one side and six on the other side of the altar was extinguished as an Alabado was sung, until only one remained.

There was a rumble like heavy timber. Everyone licked his tongue and looked up in frightened suspense; then the last remaining candle was extinguished . All of His followers had defected. He had died alone. His rapid descent into the netherworld had begun. The pipes shrieked, echoing His agonies; chains rattled and pounded, and clanked, symbolizing the liberation of

His soul. The heavy thumping of boulders falling symbolized the earthquake,(26) and the opening of graves of the saints. The pandemonium kept increasing like giant breakers in terrifiyng and deafening crescendos.

There were loud cries of terror as the dead symbolically rose. The hellish maddening roar increased in apocalyptic fury for about an hour, an hour that seemed an eternity, as the wild wind outside shrieked and tore at the shutters and the old tin roof as though they were echoing in violent fear and protest, cursing their inanimate state. Without portent, there was just as deafening a silence.

The Penitentes lit their lanterns as everyone sighed in grateful relief; looking around to see if they were still alive, and surprised that they were still whole after such a dreadful and frightening experience. The terrible moment had come and gone. The Penitentes broke the silence with song as they backed away from the altar, and disappeared out the door and into the darkness. Their lanterns swaying rhythmically reminded us that our Saviour was deep in His tomb, and that only the awful hush of a great loss and tragedy remained.

As we returned to our homes along the little road on the edge of the cliff the twinkling lights of the cities below and faraway glistened like myriads of stars in a sable sky, lent perspective to our experience. It was a journey through the ages, a moment in eternity.

The gleaming lights of Los Alamos, the Atom City on an invisible mesa in the darkness, on the mountains in the distance portended that this is today, but the swaying lanterns of the Penitentes, as they disappeared around the bend in the road ahead and their tragic chorus echoed by the lament of the wild winds said, "Yes, today, tomorrow, and all of the yesterdays are here today and forever."

fin

A DIOS! A DIOS! A DIOS!

WEEP WITH BITTER TEARS

HE MERELY LOVED

LOVE ENDURETH ALL

Amen Sin Jesus

BILL TATE

TRUCHAS

Rio Grande SUN, Espanola, N.M., June 25, 1970

(**Editor's Note**: Bill Tate, author of the book "Penitentes of the Sangre de Cristos," wrote the following account of the death of Miguel Archibeque, Hermano Supremo of the Penitentes, for the SUN)

—O—

## MIGUEL ARCHIBEQUE
### Hermano Mayor Supremo
### Los Hermanos de Nuestro
### Padre Jesus Nazareno

The lantern has entered the house, because he is no longer here.

Miguel Archibeque, Hermano Mayor Supremo of the Penitentes was laid to rest in the little village of San Miguel, in the quiet valley of the Rio Pecos, where he was born 86 years ago.

Miguel Archibeque, gave almost an entire lifetime of service to the Holy Brotherhood, of which he was an important part. He was the best friend they ever had, because it was he who united all the moradas in the mountains as one brotherhood.

After endless tireless years of pilgrimmage visiting the isolated mountain sanctuaries, he persuaded the Brothers of the Sangre de Cristos to accept a common set of ordinances and bylaws.

It was a long procession of setbacks and sorrows, but he accepted them as a gift; his cross and crown, but his gentle smile and soft eyes showed he bore his burden well.

Success finally came to Miguel, when in 1947, the late Archbishop Byrne pronounced the blessing and the protection of the Church on the Order of the Penitentes.

In 1958 Dr. Reginald Fisher of the New Mexico Historical Society and Archbishop Byrne presented him with an autographed copy of the beautiful hand illuminated volume of The Way of the Cross, the alabados of the Penitentes, as an honorarium for his labors.

Mr. Archibeque was born in San Miguel on the 1st of July, 1883. He attended school there. His father died when he was only a small boy, so he went barefoot, and wore shirts made of flour sacks.

His mother ground corn on a matate, and he carried firewood from the mountains on his back, to help support his small brothers and sisters. During Holy Week of the year of 1910 Miguel entered the Order of the Penitentes.

Governor Dave Cargo, speaking in deep emotional tones, in his eulogy for Mr. Archibeque said "he made an enormous impact on New Mexico, particularly the northern part. Few people were aware of his influence."

Archbishop Davis added that, "Miguel Archibeque was very instrumental in bringing some very good leadership into the Penitentes."

Beside the coffin stood a standard emblazoned with Jesus bearing His cross and the legend "Concilio Supremo."

Members of the brotherhood sang the Alabados, the sad and sacred songs of the Penitentes, that were so dear to him. The brothers spoke of him as "Mi hermano Miguel."

It is said his successor has been named. He is M. Santos Melendez, who lives in Albuquerque.

## FOOTNOTES

1. **Penitente**
   Secret religious group in muntains of Northern New Mexico, and Southern Colorado.

2. **Las Truchas, The Trouts**
   The fish is the symbol of Christian Missionaries. Named in memory of the martyrs who first brought the Gospel to the Indians of Spanish America.

3. **Sangre de Cristo, Blood of Christ**
   The Cross of the Penitentes.
   The snow crosses on the faces of the Truchas Peaks.

4. **To Worship in Secret, see Matthew Chap. 6.**

5. **Rosario, Rosary**
   The collection of Ave Marias and Padre Nuestros said at once, and counted by the beads of a rosary.

6. **Alabados, Hymns**
   Sung in praise of the Sacrament.

7. Semana Santa, Holy Week

8. Morada, Abode of the Cristo. Meeting place of Penitentes. Contains a chapel complete with altar, and a secret inner chamber for the celebration of The Last Supper and secular meetings, etc.

9. Saints in the Valleys by Jose Espinosa. UNM Press.

10. See Franciscans and St. Francis Ency Brit.

11. See Donaldson's Theatre of the Greeks, Geo. Bell and Sons 1879, John William Donaldson D.D.

12. Spain, Spanish Literature, Ency Brit.

13. Theresa, St. Ency Brit.

14. Carmelites, Ency Brit.

15. John, St., of the Cross, Ency Brit.

16. Avila and Castile, Ency Brit.

17. Tertiaries, Ency Brit.

18. Santos, Mitchell Wilder and Edgar Breitenbach. The Taylor Museum, Colorado Springs Fine Art Center

19. USSR, Early Russian Icons, Victor Lasarell and Otto Demus New York Graphic Society.

20. Calvary, or Golgotha, the place of a skull. Mark Chap. 15 Verse 22. A public cemetery on a mount or a hill. Where Jesus was crucified also the sepulchre of Joseph of Arimatha. His buria lplace.

21. Calvario, a large cross, designating Calvary. See 20.

22. The Crosses of the Mountains, huge glacial formed crosses on the sides of the Truchas Peaks, each abouť 2,000 ft. or more in length. It was after these the Sangre de Cristo Mountains were named by the early day explorers in the 16th Century.

23. The Holy Supper, Luke 22.

24. A wooden rattle consisting of a ratchet on a handle with two vibrating sticks in a wooden case, when spun makes a roar. Used by medieval churches during Lent or funerals in lieu of bells.

25. One who leads the prayers and singing.

26. The earthquake, Matthew Chap. 27.

## BIBLIOGRAPHY

Bibliographies are compiled for various reasons. The titles listed herein are for reference purposes only and are not necessarily recommended. Most of them are unfavorable to the Penitentes, or place them in a bizarre or a lurid light. Many are sheer propaganda, and as such are distorted for the author's own purpose, what ever that may be. Never the less, they may be helpful to the reader or researcher who desires to pursue the subject further.

Abreau, Margaret: Three r's Plus, N. Mex. Mag., Oct. '63.

Adams, Eleanor, The Penitente Brothers, Sunset, April 17.

Ahlborn, Richard E., The Penitente Moradas of Abiquiu, Smithsonian Institution Press, 1968.

Andalusia, Portrait of. Produced by Deben BhattaRya LP Argo Records, Decca, 115 Fulham Rd., London, SW3. England.

Applegate, Betty, Los Hermanos Penitentes, Southwest Review Oct. 31.

Aulnoy d' Countess, Relation du Voyage d' Espagne 1692, Vol II, pp 158-164.

Austin, Mary, The Trail of Blood, Century Mag., May '24.

Austin, Mary, The Land of Journey's Ending, p349-72, Allen & Unwin, London 1924.

Bach, Marcus: Crucifixion by Request, Christian Century, 10 Mar'37.

Bach, Marcus: Faith and My Friends, p151-94, Bobbs-Merrill, '51.

Bach, Marcus: Strange Sects and Curious Cults, Dodd, Mead & Co., New York, NY.

Bandelier, Adolph, Southwestern Journals of, UNM Press Albuquerque, 1966.

Barbet, Pierre, A Doctor at Calvary Image, Garden City, NY '63.

Barker, George: Some Aspects of Penitential Processions in Spain, and The American Southwest, Journal of American Research V70 No. 276, P137-42.

Barker, S. Omar: Los Penitentes, Overland, April '24.

Barton, Rev. W. E. DD: The Penitentes of New Mexico, Congregational Education Society, Boston.

Beck, Warren A.: New Mexico, A History of Four Centuries, Univ. of Okla. Press, Norman, P21, 122, 205, 218, 225, 292, 232.

Benavides, Fr. Alonso: Memorial of 1630, Horn and Wallace, Albuquerque, p2, 211.

Bergman, Ingmar: The Seventh Seal, Simon Ted Schuster, 1966.

Beshoar, B. B., Western Trails To Calvary. The Westerners, Denver, 1950.

Boyd, E. Los Hermanos Penitentes, a review El Palacio, vol. 76 No. 3

Boyd, E., The New Mexico Santero, El Palacio, Spring, 1969, Museum of New Mexico.

Bright, Robt., Life and Death of Little Joe, Doubleday, 1944.

Bunting, Bainbridge and John Conron, The Architecture of Northern New Mexico, NM Architecture, Sept. Oct. '66.

Burma, John H.: Los Hermanos Penitentes, Duke University Press, 1954.

Burns, John H.: Los Hermanos Penitentes, A Case Study of the Cultural Survival of Flagellation, '54, p188-198.

Burton, Fay: The Devil and The Penitente, N. Mex. Mag. April '33.

Carr, Lorraine, To The Phillipines With Love, Sherbourne Press, Los Angeles '66.

Catholic Encyclopedia Vol. XI Published 1911. Aurelio Espinosa.

Cather, Willa.: Death Comes To The Archbishop, A. Knopf.

Cervantes, Don Quixote.

Chase, C. M., New Mexico and Colorado 1881, Frontier Book, Ft. Davis, Texas.

Chavez, Fr. Angelico: Archives of the Archdiocese of Santa Fe. Academy of American Franciscan History, Washington, D.C.

Chavez, Fr. Angelico: The Penitentes of New Mexico, New Mexico Historical Review, April '54, p97-123.

Coke, Van Deren, A Note On B. J. O. Nordfeldt's "Penitente Crucifixion", Art Museum Bulletin, University of New Mexico. No. 2 Spring, 1967.

Cordova, Lorenzo de, Echoes of the Flute, Ancient City Press, Santa Fe, 1972.

Cubells, Joseph, Rev. Fr., Holy Family Parish, Family Life Magazine, Fall '67.

Darley, Alexander M.: The Passionates of the Southwest, or The Holy Brotherhood, a Revelation of the Penitentes, Pueblo, 1893.

Desert Golgotha, Literary Digest, 3 April, '37.

Dickey, Roland: New Mexico Village Arts, UNM Press, Albuquerque, P122, 156-157, 180-182, 250.

Dublin. Review, V.

Eight Great Tragedies: A Mentor Book. New American Library '57.

Eisenstein, Que Viva Mejico (Film).

Ellis. Florence Hawley, Passion Play in New Mexico, New Mexico Quarterly, Summer '52.

Ellis, Richard N,, New Mexico Past and Present, UNM Press, Albuquerque, 1971.

El Palacio V3 No. 4 p31, V4 p60, V8 p2-21.

Espanola and its Environs Harper's Magazine May 1885, Reprinted by Rio Grande SUN, Espanola. N.M.

Espinosa, Jose E., Saints In The Valleys, UNM Press '60 Alb. P32-33, 52, 54, 74-75, 80, 85, 87.

Fere Revue de Medicine, August, 1900.

Ferguson, Erna: Our Southwest p254, Alfred A. Knopf.

Fergusson, Harvey: Rio Grande, Wm. Morrow, NY, p79, 116, 124, 211, 218, 219, 220, 226.

Fisher Reginald, Notes on the Relations of the Franciscans to the Penitentes, El Palacio, Dec. 41.

Fisher, Reginald: The Way of The Cross, NM School Amer. Research '58.

Five Continents Catalog, 1965, Folk Art Museum, Museum of New Mexico, Santa Fe.

Flynn, D. J., Holy Week With the Penitentes, Harper's Weekly 26 May, 1894.

Forrest, Earl: Missions and Pueblos of the Southwest '24, p195-206.

Foster, George, Confradia and Compadrazgo in Spain and Spanish America, Southwestern Journal of Anthropology, 1953.

Foster, Joseph: In the Night I Sing, Scribners '42.

Gaastra, Bonney R., The Doorways of Penitente Land Architectural Record, Feb. 25.

George, David, The Flamenco Guitar, Society of Spanish Studies, Madrid, 1969.

Godoy, Armand, The Drama and the Passion.

Grant, Blanche, Taos Today, Press of the Pioneers, New York '25.

Grant, Blanche: When Old Trails Were New, Press of The Pioneers, New York '34.

Gregg, Josiah: Commerce of The Prairies, Univ. of Okla Press '58.

Hall, Perilous Sanctuary.

Haystad, Ladd: Triple Cities, N. Mex. Hist Journal Nov. '28, p9-11.

Heald, Weldon: The Spanish Missions of New Mexico, Arizona Quarterly, Spring '56. p61-70.

Henderson, Alice Corbin: Brothers of Light, Harcourt '37.

Henderson, Alice C., Calvary in New Mexico, Readers Digest March '40.

Hernandez, Juan: Cactus Whips & Wooden Crosses, Journal of American Folklore, July-Sept. '63, p216-224.

Hewitt, Edgar L.: Mission Monuments of New Mex., UNM Press '43.

Hogue, Alexandre, Land of Little Churches, El Palacio, 30 Mar '29.

Hogue, Jo, Miguel Archibeque, El Penitente Supremo, Santa Fe News, 15 Jan. '70.

Hogue, Jo Roybal, The Penitentes: Unique New Mexico Easter Rites, New Mexican, 11 April, 1971, Santa Fe.

Holben, Richard, The Man Who Paints the Penitentes (Bill Tate), Empire, Denver Post, 15 April, 1973.

Holy Bible, New Testament
    St. Matthew, Chapters 26 and 27
    St. Mark, Chapters 14 and 15
    St. Luke, Chapters 22 and 23
    St. John, Chapters 18 and 19

Horgan, Paul: Great River, The Rio Grande in North American History, Rinehart. NY, '54, p379-382.

Horgan, Paul: The Centuries of Santa Fe, E. P. Dutton, '56, p314.

Horka-Follick, Lorayne, Los Hermanos Penitentes, Western Lore Press, Los Angeles, '69.

Howath, O. H., "The Survival of Corporal Punishment" Journal Anthropological Institute Feb. 1889.

Huxley, Aldus, Brave New World.

Hyneck, R. W. MD: Science & The Holy Shroud, Benedictine Press, Pilsen Station, Chicago, '36.

Ingersoll, Ernest, Crest of The Continent, R. R. Donnelley, Chicago, 1889 pp94-95.

Jaramillo, Cleofas: Shadows of the Past, p63-65. Ancient City Press, Santa Fe, New Mexico.

Kazantzakis, Nikos, The Greek Passion, Simon and Schuster.

Kenney, Ida Louise, Cross Bearers of New Mexico, Overland, Sept. '10.

Keshishian, John M., Vivid Account of Mysterious Sect, Kansas City Star, 21 April, 1973.

Konapak, Farona: Hermanos Penitentes, NM Mag. March '33.

Kubler, George: Religious Architecture of New Mexico, Rio Grande Press, Chicago, '62, p142.

Kubler, George Santos, Catalog, Amon Carter Museum of Western Art, June, 1964.

La Farge, Oliver: Santa Fe, p149-50, 331-32, Univ of Okla '59.

Lambert, Fred: The Penitentes, True West Mag, May-June '63.

Laughlin, Ruth: Caballeros, Caxton Printers Ltd '45, Caldwell, Idaho, p216-17, 330.

Laxalt, Robt., New Mexico The Golden Land, National Geographic, Sept., 1970.

Lea, Aurora Lucero-White: Folklore Hispanic Southwest, p219-22, Naylor Co., San Antonio.

Little World Apart, S. Omar Barker, Doubleday, 1966.

Leonard, George B. A. Different Journey-Mexico, Look, 3 Feb. '69.

Le Viness, W. Thetford: Pathway to Penitente Rites, Desert, April '60.

Le Viness, W. Thetford: He Carves The Santos, Desert Jan. '58.

Le Viness, The Truth About the Penitentes, Empire, Denver Post, 22 March 1970.

Penitentes Literary Digest, 15 May '20.

Los Hermanos Penitentes, El Abogado Cristiano, Mexico City, 15 Nov., 1890.

Los Hermanos Penitentes, El Palacio, 31 Jan., '20.

Los Penitentes, Overland, Apr '24.

Ledesma, Gabriel Fernandez, El Triunfo de la Muerte, Procession in New Mexico, Mexico en el Arte, Nov. '48.

Lummis, Chas Fletcher: Land of Poco Tiempo, Scribners, 1893.

Lummis, Chas F., An American Passion Play, Land of Sunshine, May '96.

Lummis, Chas Fletcher: Mesa, Canon, and Pueblo, pl, 22-28.

MacGill, Fergus: Brotherhood in Blood, Real Mag, June '66.

Marriott, Alice: Maria The Potter of San Ildefonso, Univ of Okla Press '55, p42-51.

May, Florence: The Penitentes, Nat Hist, Dec. '36.

Michener, James, Iberia, Fawcett Crest Books, Random House.

Mills, George: Lucifer & The Crucifer, Taylor Museum, Colo Sprinas.

Morgan, Monroe: Brothers in an Ancient Faith, Desert. April '50.

Morgan, Willard D., Through Penitente Land With a Leica Camera,

N.M. Mag., Feb. '29.

Morgan, Willard D., Where 16th Century Customs Linger, Bureau Farmer, April '30.

Mazulla, Fred & Jo, Through the Dark Hours, Empire Denver Post, 22 March, 1970.

New Mexico Federal Writers Project, Hastings House '62, p123-4.

Newsweek, 15 Feb. '36.

Nohl, Johannes: The Black Death, Ballantine Books, NY, '60.

Odendahl, Eric M., Saint or Devil? True West, March-April, 1967.

Otero, Miguel A., My Life on the Frontier, Press of the Pioneers, '39.

Otis, Raymond: Medievalism in America, N Mex Quarterly V36-'36.

Penitent Brothers, Cosmopolitan, May, 1889.

Penitential Rite of the Ancient Mexicans, Zelia Nuttal, Peabody Museum, Cambridge, 1904.

Photography Annual - 1971, Good Friday in Bercanos, Spain, by Rafael Souz Lobato.

Prince, L. Bradford: Spanish Mission Churches of New Mexico p363-73.

Rael, Juan: New Mexico Spanish Feasts, Calif. Folklore Quarterly, Jan. '42.

Rael, Juan: The New Mexico Alabados, Stanford Univ Press. '59.

Regoyos, de, Dario, Espanola Negra, 1899, p71.

Revista Catolica, Las Vegas, N.M. 1875 to 1910 and 1886-1890.

Revista de Revistas, Mexico, 14 April '63.

Riding, William H., A Trail In The Far Southwest, Harpers New Monthly Magazine, June 1876.

Salpointe, Rev. John Baptist, Soldiers of the Cross, Calvin Horn Publisher, p161-163.

Santos, George Kubler: Amon Carter Museum, Ft. Worth.

Saunders, Lyle: A Guide to Materials on Cultural Relations in New Mexico p2, 7, 1923, 3258, 3337, 3392, 3447, 3497, 3502, 3509, 3527, 3531, 3544, 3548, 3559, 3561, 3583, 3651, 3684, 3693, 3698, 3822, 4834.

Scarlett, Conrad: The Hermit of El Porvenir, N Mex Hist Journal Dec. '30.

Scott, Winfield Townley, The Still Young Sunlight, The Vanishing American, 1947.

Segale, Sister Blandina: At The End of the Santa Fe Trail, Bruce Publishing Co., Milwaukee, p41-42.

Shalkop, Robert L.: Wooden Saints, Taylor Museum, Colo. Springs.

Simmons, Marc, Charles Lummis and Amado Chaves, San Marcos Press.

Sinclair, John I.: Singers of The Night, Westways Mag, Los Angeles.

St. John of the Cross, Dark Night of the Soul, Image, Garden City, NY, 1959.

St. John of the Cross, Ascent of Mount Carmel, Image, Garden City, NY, 1958.

St. John of the Cross, Complete Works of, Newman Press, 1964.

St. Teresa of Avila, The Autobiography of, Image, Garden City, NY, 1960.

Sticca, Sandro, The Latin Passion Play, origins & development, NYU Press, Albany, NY, '70.

Stravinsky, La Sacre due Printempo.

Sylvester, Harry: Dayspring, Appleton-Century '45.

Tate, Bill: Mountain Chants of the Sangre de Cristos, Tate Gallery Publications, Truchas, New Mexico, '70.

Tate, Bill: Truchas Village With A View, Tate Gallery Publications, Truchas, N.M. '69.

Tayor, C. Bryson, Mexican Penitentes of New Mexico, Everybody's Magazine, Apr. 1904.

Taylor, Carl N., Agony in New Mexico, Today, 15 Feb. '36.

Theatre Arts, April '38, T. W. Stevens.

The Trail of Blood, Century Magazine, May '24.

Theil, Al P. Calvary in New Mexico, Sun Trails Mag Vol 6 No. 4.

Tibetan Book of The Dead, W. Y. Evans-Wentz-Oxford Press, N.Y.

Time Magazine, 9 Mar., '36 Blood in New Mexico.

Time Magazine, 3 April, '37 Desert Golgotha.

Townsend, Joseph, A Journey Through Spain, 1786 Vol I p122, Vol III p15.

Townsend, Richard Baxter: Tenderfoot in New Mexico '24, p48-53.

Tschursin, Lisa, Los Hermanos Penitentes, Pvt. Ptg., Washington, DC, 1973.

Trimble, Walter, Truchas: Village With a View and its Poet Lureate, Bill Tate: Poet, Painter & Philosopher, Encanto Magazine, Albuquerque, N.M.

Udell, Isaac: The Penitentes, Cosmopolitan Art Gallery, Denver.

Udell, Isaac: South Dakota Review.

United Press, Good Friday Drama, Berkeley Gazette, 26 Mar '48.

Uncle Sam's Medieval Citizens And Their Passion Play, Literary Digest, 15 May '20.

Vigil, Cleofas, Singer, New Mexican Alabados, LP recording, Taos Recordings, Publications, Taos, New Mexico.

Wallis, Michael, The Time Was Right, El Independiente, 20 Apr '73.

Walsh, William Thomas, St. Teresa of Avila, Bruce, Milwaukee, '48.

Walsingham, "Master of the Rolls" Collection Vol 1, p275, England.

Waters, Frank: People of the Valley, Alan Swallow Denver.

Waters, Frank, The Colorado, Rhinehart & Co., '46.

Waters, Frank, Conversations With, Swallow Press, Chicago, 1971.

Watters, Mary, The Penitentes: A Folk Observance, Social Forces, Dec. '27.

Weiale, Marta, The Penitentes of the Southwest, Ancient City Press, Santa Fe, New Mexico, '70.

Western Folklore, Good Friday Drama, July '48.

White, Aurora Lucero: Los Hispanos, Alan Swallow, Denver '47, p19-25.

Wilder, Mitchell A.: Santos, the Religious Folk Art of New Mexico, '43. The Taylor Museum, Colorado Springs.

Zephyrin, Fr., Father Zephyrin & The Penitentes, El Palacio, Apr '20.

Newspapers: SFNM Review April 3, 1885. SFNM Daily April 24, 1886. SFNM Review Aug. 9, 1894. SFNM Daily April 15, 1908, SFNM 8 April '55. NMex Lobo Albu 7 Oct '65. El Crepusculo, Taos Mar '56, Rio Grande SUN. Oct. 1962, Alb. Tribune, 20 Apr. '62, 24 Mar '67, SFNM 6 April '69, Espanola Exp., 27 Aug. '70.

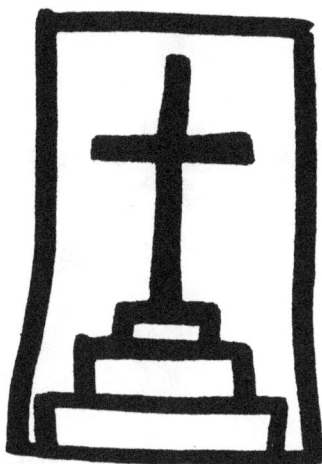

The Cross on a pediment of 3 steps. It is used to represent The Cross on Calvary. These are seen on Penitente altars in the Morada. Also the number thirteen in Chinese calligraphy.

St. Andrew's Cross, upon which St. Andrew suffered a martyr's death symbolizing that its bearers are prepared to make a like sacrifice.

(The Tao.)

## THE HOST AND CHALICE
Carved at the junction of a Penitente Calvario, located in Las Truchas. This is a very early Christian symbol. It is an "X" imposed on the Cross. The arrows since antiquity have represented the authority of God. The Cup is to catch and preserve Christ's blood. It represents the Penitentes as the conservators of the Faith.

The Cross and 4 nails. It was also used by the Copts.

**LA CARRETA DE LA MUERTE**
by BILL TATE                    Photo By DICK SPAS

**BILL TATE**　　　　**TRUCHAS**

www.ingramcontent.com/pod-product-compliance
Lightning Source LLC
Chambersburg PA
CBHW031152090426
42738CB00008B/1299